THE BLACKNESS IN ME

POETIC LESSONS OF LIFE FROM CLEVELAND TO ACCRA

WRITTEN BY:

MICHELLE DORNOR

COPYRIGHT

Printed in the United States of America

First Printing, 2022

Special Edition, JUNETEETH 2022

Dornor Consulting Publishing

Cheyenne, Wyoming

http://dornorconsulting.services

Dedication

To the little Black girl in me who never gave up and dared to think she could, so she did...

Why I wrote this book

Akwaaba! Means welcome in the Akan language of Ghana. I wrote this book to share my experiences of growing up as a Black woman in the ghettos of America to traveling the world and walking through the door of return while visiting the homeland of my ancestors, Mama Africa... West Africa, Ghana.

MY ASK

My hope is that the words contained herein will encourage your spirit to pursue your highest good and purpose. If the words herein have touched you in some way please leave a positive review & share on your social media pages with the hashtag:

#theblacknessinme

With Love, Michelle

TABLE OF CONTENTS

Dedication	3
Yellow Heffa	5
Black !*#@%	7
Between 2 Worlds	9
Dear Black Woman	11
But Why Tho?	12
Shut up Black Girl	14
Hate	16
The Project	19
Stay Black & Die	21
Blame it on the Culture	23
The Talk	25
We Still Slaves	30
Where they do that at?	32
I had to leave it alone	34
Anyone	36
Gettin' it in	37
Freedom	40
Hood Rich	41
Soul Food	43
Drum For Me	45
Africa Song	46
My Warring Days are Over	48
Black Eve	50

YELLOW HEFFA

Yellow Heffa

Coming to take our man

Coming to take our place

Coming to fake the race

Skin as yellow as a banana

Lighter than a brown paper bag

Come here yellow Heffa

Let us tug at your long hair don't care

And red mark your face

Let's finish the job

Of the rape committed against your Dark Ancestor

That made your skin so light

Almost white

And that is why we hate you

And call you Yellow Heffa

Because we do not recognize

That you are still our sister

And that you need love and not lust or hate too

The author's personal self-photo, Michelle Dornor

BLACK !*#@%

Out of all the names you can call me

You decide to call me that

Because my melanin glows

Brighter

Stronger

Shining like gold

But you call me that

Due to my darker pigmentation

And your hesitation

To recognize that I am Queen Mother of the Earth

Ruler of the Sun

Yes I am the one

They call the 7 daughters of Eve

My skin has been blessed by the Gods

Kissed by the Ancestors

So if you didn't know

You betta ask somebody

Free Use Photo Courtesy of 3Motional Studio via Pexels.com

BETWEEN TWO WORLDS

Caught in the middle

Not white enough

Too light

Not dark enough

Too dark

Being tossed to and fro

My hair twirls and curls

But they say it's not a fro

Not being dark enough

Has been my lifetime woe

But too dark for the likes of some

Who tell me not to come back this way no mo

So I learned to be alone

Not knowing where I fit in

The boys just want to use me

Cause my skin and hair is "pretty"

But what is pretty

When this kind of treatment makes you feel so ugly

And the girls they hate me

And wish I would melt away from their cold stares

They just glare and glare

But I act as if I don't care

Till I get home to my room

Stare out the window

And wonder will it ever get better

I find my solace in writing

It's the only place I am accepted

And does not care what I look like

Author photo of window 2nd floor of Elmina Slave Castle, Cape Coast, Ghana

DEAR BLACK WOMAN

Some say we have attitude

Some say we wear a frown

Some say we are inadequate

When on our heads

There is a crown

Of glory

Of splendor

We only need

To surrender

Our tough exterior

That we have used

To feel superior

Made to believe

We are not enough

You are enough

My Sister

You were born to achieve

Whatever your heart desires

Fan the flames & stoke the fire

That's deep within

Regardless of what you've been told

You

Can

Win

BUT WHY THO?

Why do you love our men

But scared of us?

Why do you love our men

But jealous of us?

Don't you know

The Black woman has died a million deaths

To give birth to the men

Who die to be with you!

While they claim to love their mother

Yet don't honor the womb that gave birth to him

Why do you love our men

But don't want to be our friend

Why do you love our men

But yet won't give us a smile or a grin

Why do you love our men

But treat us as a sin

If seen in their company

Free Use Photo courtesy of Jennifer Enujiugha via Pexels.com

SHUT UP BLACK GIRL

Who told you to speak Black girl

Who told you that you are beautiful Black girl

Who told you that you are intelligent Black girl

Who told you to encourage yourself Black girl

Who told you to believe you are special Black girl

Why you so angry Black girl

You are not making any sense Black girl

Oh?

What was that we just heard…

You called yourself a hoe, a b!*#@% Black girl

Well, we will back you up on that Black girl

Permission to speak

But only to speak against yourself …

Black girl

HATE

From the green lush bushes and trees far away

On the continent of Africa

To the Amazon River in South America

My ancestors long ago used to be free

Controlling their own destiny

They made war

Slaves were their payment

But mistreat them no

They would become family

Integration

Even marrying one another until the slave of war became free

No lifelong slavery

One had the true promise of release

While maintaining his dignity

But that all changed

When the unknown powers

Gave birth to power and greed

It was no longer warring tribes

It was a game of a different kind

Conquest of the mind

Making a people change their minds

While they robbed the mines

And made us give up

What was once universal

Yours and mine

Freedom and security

Were to no longer be

We were changed from humans to commodities

Just some man's property

Listed with no name on paper

Right along with the sheep and cattle

Still today our life really doesn't matter

Punishment has changed

From whips, lynchings, and chains

To not even allowed to speak peacefully

There is nothing gained

Because the sound of our voice

Is like a rushing mighty water

That disturbs the status quo

And brings to mind the pain and guilt felt from long ago

Like a wound that never heals

Racism is an infection

Hatred becomes terrorism

That can no longer be dealt with

It must be cut off

So we scream and we shout

We cry and we wail about

Why why why

Are we still hunted

Still hated

Still not free

Only as free as the powers want us to be

Free Use photo by Ramphoko Mahula via Pexels.com

THE PROJECT

The projects was a project

And the subject was people like I

And people like you

People like we

People like us

And they built walls

So we could learn to build walls of our own

To keep them from coming in

While so many of us wanted to get out

But couldn't get out

Our prison was mental

And we were served a life sentence

Because we were different

Because we were powerful

Creative Intelligent

And the stupidity of this project

Did exactly what it was supposed to do

Make us dumber and dumber

Yearn and linger

Hanging on corners

With no purpose

No drive

No plan

And nothing to drive

To drive us out of the raggedy mind state

Stumbling in the dark

Don't even know what is making us stumble

Don't even think to turn the lights back on…

Ooh child

They say things are gonna get better

But you better

Not think more highly of yourself

That you are good enough to climb the wall

Escape from a project that you were never meant to be in

If you go within

You can win

But here comes that project manager again

Telling you who do you think you are

Get back where you belong

And you go

Cause you never did belong out there

And now the projects

Feels like home

So you never leave

Never think to roam

And you settle down into a life of mediocrity

Spending your days and nights on the phone

Talking bout I'm from the projects man!

While never owning a project of your own

STAY BLACK AND DIE

I wanted economic freedom

But you gave me welfare

The projects and roaches

I wanted peace of mind

And you took a piece of my mind

When I looked at the college tuition

And realized

I had better change my mind

After looking at that price

This world wasn't made for me

I just better stay black and die

I wanted some tranquility

So I worked real hard to fit in

I changed my speech

I changed my clothes

Why most even change their nose

But even though we all knows

That no matter how educated

Its still a no's go

I just better stay black and die

I wanted some dreams to come to fruition

So I mustered up all my ambition

Just to realize that its useless

When you told me

Im pretty good at being black

So I better just stay black and die

But not I

I will stay black

But I'm

Going to live

Going to grow

Going to speak

Going to shout

Going to preach

Going to lecture

Going to teach

To stay black

And live…

Yes

To live.

BLAME IT ON THE CULTURE

She grew up where people didn't take her things

But she grew up where people took the things that were meant to be hers

But were not entrusted to her yet

So she never even got to hold them

She learned to put her dreams on hold

No…

Up for sale to the lowest bidder

To dream was to fail

And yet you wonder why can't she think positive?

She grew up believing that all Black women had no hair of their own

So she questioned the length of that beautiful brown sister

But fully believing that the Caucasian with long flowing locks woke up like that

Which continue to feed the stereotype that

All Black women are angry

When she gets angry from being wrongly pigeonholed by a stranger

Who knows nothing personal about her

That sister grew up seething with rage

Because speaking up meant losing her job or going to jail

While the other grew up privileged to say whatever she pleased

It was a sign of emotional intelligence

The inquisition was lawful to her and still is

Just mere curiosity that must be solved at the expense of others

Never realizing the expense of others when bias is spewed in their face

Exposure is a necessity

Minding your own business is a must

Treating others with dignity is the highest good

Not just reciting in God we trust

I just felt a bit of disgust

For I feel that we just

Should blame it on the culture

For teaching us to be devils

While we leave our angel wings in the heavens

Which we shall never attain

THE TALK

Again.

I go to bed with dreams of rainbows and sunshine

To be awakened by

Screams and the crack of a collar bone

Flashes of lightning and rolling thunder

Sweat and anguish from a long-ago event

So my day starts with mourning and sadness

That I have to shake off

Because its Monday

I have to go to work

And I can't let nobody know

About that time when…

That time???

What about…

Now?

What about all the …

Fears

Insecurities

Post Traumatic Stress

Repressed memories

The depression

That hijacks my mind

When my subconscious takes over

I didn't ask for this

I didn't plant these seeds

But it's mine to grapple with

Whether I like it or not

And Daddy and Mommy…

It's not their fault

They didn't plant those seeds either

And neither did my grandfather

Or grandmother

Or Big Momma and Big Daddy

Or Me maw

Or great great granddaddy Williams

Or any of my ancestors

Because I have Black skin

At some point, the woman and the man

That I came from was stolen from their own precious land

Taught to forget

Forget your name

Forget your family

Forget your history

Forget your values

Forget your country

Forget your God

And worshiped the one that they were commanded to worship

They couldn't not even think about leaving a legacy!

I mean, how could they?

My ancestors had wounds as deep as the ocean

Wounds from beatings

Wounds from killings

Wounds from the training and the teaching

From a Mother and Son being forced to make babies

From watching their Father, Brother, Son be publicly sodomized to break his unrelenting spirit

Finally, he was broken

No longer a man

But a boy

Who whimpers in the night when no one is watching

From the woman feeling the sting of the Ma'am of the Big House's hand

Because the Ma'am's husband snuck down from the house to the cabin again

No use in cryin'

She must not let her milk dry up

Because the Ma'am's baby gonna need feeding again soon

Learning to take care of everything else

Except for her own

That is why the Black woman is "affectionately" called

Momma this and Momma that

What about Ma'am?

Lady?

Woman?

What about Beautiful Soul?

Not allowed to make her own path or build anything of her own

From the child too young to know

But was ripped from the womb that cradled him or her

To survive was to forget that you belonged to someone

To forget that someone did love you … somewhere

Because the pain of remembering is too much

So the child learns to put on a tough exterior to shield the pain

And live life not needing anything

Or anyone

So the man learns to act like a subservient little boy

And the woman takes care of everybody like a man does and forgets how and what it feels like to be a lady who has her own dreams and goals

And the child

Rebellious and ready to set the world on fire

From repressed memories of having a family

That were no more than like ghosts in the wind…

Don't learn to read

And speak broken English so they don't assume intelligence

Or that you even know how to talk

Yes

All of this and more

Were passed down to me

And it has taken all my life

To finally begin life

Now that I am planning for and halfway at the end

Self-medicating and Self-teaching

Because there is no counselor

Who truly understands

The dynamics, the legacy that has been handed down

From the lessons of slavery

So many thick layers

Where do we even begin?

The answer is … we don't know because there's so much

And too many centuries have gone by with no lasting help

Or permanent change

So before I can be emotionally intelligent

Before I can be rational

Before I can hear

Before I can see

Before I speak

I must be healed

I must be nourished

I must have resources

I must be loved

As I am and for who I am now

And most importantly,

I must be heard.

Free Use photo by Márcio Filho via Pexels.com

WE STILL SLAVES

Don't you want to be free

I just want to be me

Bit it makes you bad

If you want to flee

Why indentured servants

Why slavery

The sugarcane

And the cocoa

It is beyond reach

Of the mind and the soul

Which can hardly behold

The horrors untold

Of a people

Whose destinies

Never unfold

But

We still slaves

Who live for the weekend

Dying for it to be five o'clock somewhere

Trying to escape the reek

Of our body odor

From putting up with corporate nonsense

So we soothe

Our pain

By going against the grain

Of Mother Nature

And we drown ourselves in 98 bottles of beer

In hopes that our fear

Of never being free

Is erased by cheer

So we pretend to be cheerful

When we are really crying on the inside

On Friday at 5pm

Every soul cries out

Free at last!

Until Sunday night

After we sing praises to the most high

We groan

Realizing

We have to return to our real master on Monday morning…

WHERE THEY DO THAT AT?

Thank you for the holiday

It was long overdue

My ancestors are rolling over in their grave

Still hurting from the black and blue

Yeah they still giving us the blues

Saying we are never satisfied

Yeah we not satisfied

By the way

Where is our 40 acres and that mule

Where is our land

Where is our name

Where is the history

Ripped from us and replaced with shame

Am I an African American

If I never stepped foot in Africa

Why not call me a native

Seeing I was born here on this soil

I am an American

And that makes me native…

Where

Is the real change

Not just the drip

That makes me believe you changed

While the hood is still struggling for independence

A few may be independent

But not together

We spread out like butter

Unprepared for storm weather

But we got a holiday though…

I HAD TO LEAVE IT ALONE

Born in the city

Raised on Southern hospitality

Heart beating with the sound of …

BROOKLYNNNNN!!!!!

I Got that honest from my daddy

Mean muggin'

No lovin'

Foreva buggin'

Raised on them grits and butter

Didn't know a diamond

Could come from the gutter

So I had to leave it alone

I was called out

To stand out

To be free

And not be the ghetto queen

I was turning out to be

A classy queen

Who likes pink and lace

Had to learn to wipe that mean mug

Look off of my face

I had to leave it alone

Had to learn to smile thru the pain

Had to learn to make it on my own

Keep going thru sunshine and rain

Traveling thru doors

Vortexes and windowpanes

I had nothing to lose

And everything to gain

I put down my dreams of ghetto fame

Be ok with them calling me lame

I was looking for the real ones

Who put me up on game

Forget what they told you

Success was my aim

To get success

You have to do the same

As the nerdy kids in school

Who go used to you calling them names

Different year same story

If so you missed out on your glory

Im learning to walk the path

Of the ones who went before me

ANYMORE

I don't want to be mad anymore

Sad anymore

Angry

Raging like the billowing sea

Tossing and turning

Yearning to fight

I want

Peace

Sweeping over me

Into a calm mist

That carries me away to a place

Love

The foundation of life

Sets souls on fire

To a destiny

Beyond stars and lights

Into the darkness

Where I find my light

Never to be affected

By anything

Anyone

Anymore

GETTING' IT IN

Gettin' it in

Gettin' it in

Gettin' it in

Get get get

Getting' it in

Yep

And couldn't nobody tell you nothing

Head hard as a rock

Until you got rocked by life

Rocked right to sleep

Making nightmares

Out of your sweetest dreams

Shocked back to reality

Back to the beginning

Because the choices you made

Came from a state of fragility

In your mind

Why so blind

When you had those who walked before you

Walk before you

Saying hey

Don't go that way

Stay here for a little while

Don't go that way

Stay here for a little while

Don't be in a rush to grow up so fast chile

But you was getting' it in

In it to win it

Didn't know that karma would show up

And finish it

Saying back to the drawing board

Let's take it from the top

One mo' gin

When will you realize you were born to stand out

To be different

Not to fit in…

Getting' it in

Free Use photo by Matheus Natan via Pexels.com

FREEDOM

Shackled in chains I long to be free

Please someone save me from this misery

If I'm in chains

They say I put them on myself

Because I signed the dotted line

And changed to debt from wealth

What is a dollar even worth

If I can't have entertainment and mirth

A five-dollar dresser and a twenty-dollar shirt

This pain this misery I did give birth

Im broke but I spend even though it hurts

Im the engine that can for the economy

Why doesn't the machine usher a warning

Woe unto me

For it revels in my ongoing misery

And will offer me a peace of mind for a small fee

Release from mystery illness that isn't that cheap

Says the doctor who can't utter a peep

Cuz there is no cure for monetary stress

Unless you lay financial waste to rest

And get those fears of wretchedness up off of your chest

Starting wit the end in mind is certainly best

I feel the shackles breaking!

Let me put this financial wisdom to the test…

HOOD RICH

Dying to get rich

Gotta get rich quick

Don't have time to spare a dollar

I'm hood rich

Don't have a white or a blue collar

I'm hood rich

We all we got

What set you from

With this behavior

This attitude

Failure is the only outcome

Buying shoes, cars, ice, and clothes

Now I feel like I'm hood rich

And for sure only God knows

Head to toe dressed to the nines

While you are asset depleted

The rich are minding the times

Let me rewind

To times of fear and intimidation

Where coming together

Was more about action and less aggravation

Less talking more doing

Wanting to be accepted by all

Became our ruin

And now we are hood rich

With nothing to show

Except our cars, shoes, ice

And our clothes

SOUL FOOD

Take me back

To the Taste

Where my ancestors sat for hours

Resting from their labors

At the old place in the corner

Where the food made you long for home

After a long day's work

Where they butter the rice

And soak the fish

In a stew never ending

Where I use my hands as my fork

While I hear the woman beat fufu with the pestle

Oh yes!

The salmon that melts in my mouth

While the palm nut soup warms my soul

I can sit here for hours

And never go back home

Author's self portrait of her favorite Ghanaian dish, Abenkwan, a spicy palm nut soup simmered with fresh smoked salmon enjoyed with rice, fufu, or banku on location at the restaurant called Asante Home Touch in Accra, Ghana

DRUM FOR ME

Sing me a song from old

Make my body speak

While my hands

Twist and fold

Spinning round and round

Caught in a daze

Back and forth

Up and down

Speak to me

The African Way

Send the people a message

Loud and clear

For all to hear

Drum!

Drum for me!

Until the thing is done

And when the sun is set

And the day is through

I'll sing you a song

Let me drum for you

AFRICA SONG

It's calling me

Haunting me

My bones are yearning

And aching

For that African heat

Longing for vacation

I need a retreat

To a place where

Everyone looks like me

And I am free

To do as I please

As long as I respect

Myself

My neighbor

And your majesty

Sitting amongst the elders

My countrymen

Gaining wisdom beyond my years

Of experience

What kind of experience is this

That I should get to learn

Form the mistakes of someone else

And they do not walk with bowed heads

Nor shame

When I say

Tell me

The story again…

MY WARRING DAYS ARE OVER

Nope!

Those days are gone

The days where I doubt myself

Let others tell me what I'm worth

I know my worth

Wait for others to pick me

I pick me

Wait for someone to love me

No

I love me

And I love me first

Gone are the days

I love me first

Gone are the days

Where I shout

Louder for you

Then I do for myself

Where I praise everyone around my vicinity

While leaving me out

I now pay attention to me

And what's good for my health …

Mentally

Spiritually

Emotionally

Physically

Financially

It's a new day!

BLACK EVE

My womb contains secrets of the human genome

All the colors of the rainbow

A diamond

A prism of bliss and blessing

I started at one

And became many

Black woman

Proud

Out loud

Without apology

Strong

Soft

Feminine

Sexy

Everyone wants to taste of my delicacies

Everyone wants to get next to me

Everyone wishes that they were me

Black Eve

From the heavens and the stars I came to be

Queen of this land into the next one

For eternity

Free Use photograph by Bestbe Models via Pexels.com

(Page left intentionally blank)